Meadows

Meadows are mown, pastures are eaten. Without such regimes, the plant populations would change and woodland reclaim the ground.

One of the most popular sites for a wild flower garden is the lawn. This should be ideal for meadow and pastureland plants, for the grasses are usually of only moderate strength. The soil is often less rich than that around, as grass clippings are continually removed, so depleting the food store, and only the more dedicated gardeners feed a lawn generously.

CREATING THE MEADOW

First, decide how much of the lawn is to be converted to meadow, if possible locating it away from the more groomed garden near the house. The edges of the meadow can be defined with orthodox lawn or a paved path, which serves to make obvious your plan and provides a partial barrier for plants that are weeds one side and welcome community members the other. Next, strip off the turf to take away some of the most fertile top soil and remove the present population of grasses. Except on very poor soils, this reduced fertility is beneficial, as out-of-character over-lush plants are not wanted. If there are strong weeds like nettles, docks and dandelions, the whole area needs to be sprayed with weedkiller before the turf is removed.

The exposed soil is then worked with a rotovator or dug over to provide a seed bed. If dug roughly in the autumn, even very heavy clays will be broken up by winter frost and will be easier to reduce to a fine tilth in spring, when the soil temperature rises and makes it ideal for germination. Before sowing, the soil is firmed by treading or rolling and is raked. Alternatively, the work can be started in the spring, digging the ground and eliminating weeds through the summer, so that the soil is settled and ready for sowing at the end of summer or beginning of autumn when it is still warm. Extra drainage, in the form of field drains, is rarely necessary and it is

Snake's head fritillary, *Fritillaria meleagris*, is an ideal meadow plant

better to adapt the selection of plants to the site rather than the other way round.

Seed sowing is done in at least two stages. Mixtures of grasses can be bought ready-made from firms specializing in wild flower seeds, or you can make up your own from the less vigorous species. A tightly knit lawn is not the aim and the seed should be sown at a rate of ⅛–¼ oz per square yard (4–8 g/m²).

Flower mixtures from seedhouses may be of various types, often designed for different soils and situations. A mixture for a meadow can be broadcast thinly over the whole, first mixing the seed with dry sand to ensure even distribution. Otherwise, seed from packets of individual species can be sown – in irregular patches, but using short drills so that the seed germinates in straight lines to make early weeding easier. Fine seeds such as poppies and foxgloves do not need covering and will be scuffled into the top of the soil. With others, the rule is the larger the seeds the deeper they are sown, usually to the same depth as the size of the seeds, although the largest seeds can be somewhat deeper. In autumn, when the soil is moist and warm, most seeds will have germinated within a fortnight, but might take a little longer in spring.

Precautions should be taken against slugs during the first few weeks. If cats are a nuisance, some chicken wire over the surface should frustrate them. Birds may be deterred by netlon plastic

A lawn converted to a delightful meadow

A Wisley Handbook

Wild Flower
Gardening

MICHAEL JEFFERSON-BROWN

Cassell

The Royal Horticultural Society

THE ROYAL HORTICULTURAL SOCIETY

Cassell Educational Limited
Villiers House, 41/47 Strand,
London WC2N 5JE
for the Royal Horticultural Society

First published 1990
Reprinted 1992, 1994

British Library Cataloguing in Publication Data
A catalogue record for this book is available from the British Library

ISBN 0-304-31868-X

Photographs by Photos Horticultural, W H D Wince, Jacqui Hurst,
Andrew Lawson, Harry Smith Collection,
Michael Jefferson-Brown and NPK Landlife Ltd.

Phototypesetting by RGM Associates, Southport
Printed in Hong Kong by Wing King Tong Co. Ltd

Cover: field poppies and corn cockles in a Suffolk garden
in June (photograph by Jacquie Hurst)
Frontispiece: chicory, *Cichorium intybus*, a spectacular
perennial of chalk grassland
Back cover: a meadow within a garden (photographs by
W H D Wince)

Contents

Introduction

A love of wild flowers is something most of us feel, but at no other time has there been such a strong movement to invite them into our gardens. The reason for this renewed interest is that our wildlife is obviously under threat. Spraying of agricultural crops, including grass, has eliminated most of the hugely diverse range of species that used to be found throughout the countryside, as farm economics and high food yields demand ever greater efficiency. Wayside spraying by local authorities has compounded the situation. Motorways, housing developments and the construction of industrial and business sites have destroyed natural wildlife populations and communities over huge areas.

In some lowland counties, only as little as three to five per cent of land is left on which it is possible to find even common wild flowers. Scientific surveys have been undertaken to discover just how quickly and how much of the hedgerows of 1946 have been removed. The 500,000 miles of hedgerows then existing in England and Wales had been reduced to 386,000 miles by 1985 and the annual rate of loss is now 4,000 miles. In many parts of the country, the hedges were almost the last footholds for our native flora and accompanying wildlife, so the seriousness of the situation would be hard to exaggerate.

Belatedly, we are rethinking our attitudes. There is now a chance that many wild plants may be saved and, with them, a part of our heritage. Threats to our wildlife have sharpened our appreciation of the beauty and fascination in wild flowers. All gardeners can do something for the conservation cause and, in doing so, can make their own gardening more interesting and challenging.

Wild flower gardening is a form of cultivation, although the management involved is clearly different from that of most other kinds of gardening. The amount of overseeing necessary will vary according to the type of site and the inclinations of the gardener. Some may decide to grow a few native plants – perhaps one or two clumps of wild primroses – within the regime of the normally cultivated garden; more will wish to have an area set aside as a community of wild plants. Purists may want to grow only British

Hawthorn, *Crataegus monogyna*, a common native hedge plant

5

species within the wild flower garden, while others with more catholic tastes will allow a mixture of foreign and native plants. The usual idea is to create an attractive balance of plants that appear to look after themselves and to enjoy characterful plants which delight both individually and in a community. There are always surprises. Next to a common plant, we may be treasuring a rare or threatened species in a managed environment, such as a meadow, that has largely been lost in the wild.

Formerly, meadows rich in plants fell to the scythe before midsummer, but not before most species had bloomed and many had produced seed. Later growth allowed a second crop of flowers and another chance of procreation. However, almost all old meadows have been ploughed up and sown with a mixture of grasses suitable for grazing animals, selective weedkillers being used to prevent the broad-leaved plants (as opposed to the narrow-leaved grasses) from establishing themselves. To recreate the old meadow in miniature is one of the most popular forms of wild flower gardening and following a few simple guidelines will help to ensure success (see p. 15).

It is a mistake to dismiss the value of even a very small collection of wild plants. One advantage is that cross-pollination and the production of seed are more readily achieved. Insects arriving in the garden may be carrying pollen not only to your plants but to populations elsewhere, possibly in the wild. The plants are a source of food for insect life and, by growing suitable plants, many attractive insects like butterflies and moths and beneficial ones like bees can be encouraged (see also p. 53). Fungi can also look decorative and some may be picked and dried to use in flower arrangements indoors. Even the soil of the wild flower garden is important for its store of organic life.

This book suggests how wild flower gardening can fit into the garden as a whole, especially the smaller modern garden. It gives practical advice about starting from scratch, adapting different sites and using appropriate plants. There is a selection of recommended plants, with native species having priority.

Wild primroses, wood anemones and violets will enhance any garden

Starting a Small Wild Flower Garden

NATURAL FACTORS

As with any form of gardening, climate, aspect and soil have to be taken into account in wild flower gardening.

Not much can be done about the climate. However, in areas of very heavy rainfall, measures to improve soil drainage will help to widen the range of growable plants. Advantage can be taken of ground sloping to the south, where the warmer soil helps plants to start growing earlier and to be active longer, while the greater amount of sun results in a fuller ripening of wood and tissue. Similarly, the shelter provided by trees and shrubs, together with the warmth given by house walls and fences, can create useful microclimates. Avoidance of frost pockets is also helpful.

Wild plants, like garden plants, should be chosen to suit the situation. Being open to light and sunshine is important for meadow and grassland plants, just as shade and coolness are welcomed by woodland and hedgerow plants.

The main chemical soil factor is its pH rating – the level of acidity or alkalinity: on a scale 1 to 14, 7 is neutral, with the higher figures indicating increased alkalinity and the lower increased acidity. Acid soils of heathlands support a range of plants which is very different from that found in chalky soils. Weeds, such as the following, are useful indicators of the type of soil:

Weeds of acid soils
Anthemis arvensis corn chamomile
Erodium cicutarium common stork's bill
Fallopia convolvulus black bindweed
Lamium amplexicaule henbit
Mercurialis annua annual mercury
Raphanus raphanistrum wild radish
Rumex acetosella sheep's sorrel
Spergularia rubra sand spurrey
Urtica urens small nettle

Weeds of alkaline soils
Cerastium arvense field mouse-ear
C. fontanum subsp. *triviale* common mouse-ear
Daucus carota wild carrot
Fumaria officinalis fumitory
Hippocrepis comosa horseshoe vetch
Papaver rhoeas field poppy
Plantago media hoary plantain
Silene noctiflora night-flowering campion

Ox-eye daisies in the corner of a garden, with *Clematis* 'Nelly Moser' on the wall

9

While minor adjustments of pH levels can be made moderately easily, moving a complete point on the scale involves considerable effort. It is simpler to work with nature and to grow plants that are happy with the present pH levels. In practice, surveys have shown that the vast majority of garden soils are close to neutral and able to carry a broad spectrum of plants.

CHOOSING THE SITE

Very broadly, our wildflowers belong to three classes of site – woodland, grassland and wet areas – all of which are disappearing. Originally, most of the country was wooded and much of our flora is the remnant of mixed woodland. Grazed and mown grassland favoured certain other plants and, until the widespread use of chemical weedkillers, a very varied population coexisted with the grasses; then, with increased ploughing and the introduction of an arable rotation, different plants, many of them annuals, came to the fore, until selective weedkillers virtually exterminated them too. Wetland habitats and their plants have also become increasingly rare with subsidized and more efficient drainage of land.

Field bindweed, *Convolvulus arvensis*, a pretty but persistent weed

In the garden, we can reproduce these sites. Part of the lawn may become a meadow; trees, shrubbery, orchard and hedgerow can support woodland communities; pond, bog and damp areas can be used for moisture-loving plants and traditional herbaceous or mixed borders can foster a wide range of individual wild plants.

If there is a choice of sites for a wild flower garden, the poorer, less cultivated ground is better. A well cultivated vegetable plot, for instance, would be too fertile and encourage rank growth.

DEALING WITH UNWANTED PLANTS

Some very attractive wild plants can become a real menace if they invade the cultivated areas. It makes sense to isolate the wild garden or surround it with a *cordon sanitaire*, so that there is less chance of seed or stolon escaping. Mown lawn is an effective barrier between the wild and the traditionally cultivated areas. In very small gardens, it is prudent to avoid over-exuberant species, although some, like the quaking grass, *Briza media*, can be curbed by cutting the flowering heads before seed is distributed.

Gardeners define weeds as plants in the wrong place and even in wild flower gardening they present problems. Only large-scale or very bold plantings will allow some of the stronger invasive species, such as the following:

Achillea millefolium yarrow
Aegopodium podagraria ground elder
Anthriscus sylvestris cow parsley
Calystegia sepium hedge bindweed
Cirsium vulgare creeping thistle
Convolvulus arvensis field bindweed
Elymus repens couch grass
Epilobium angustifolium rosebay
   willow herb

E. montanum broad-leaved willow
   herb
Heracleum sphondylium hogweed
Petasites hybridus butterbur
Rumex species dock
Sonchus species sow thistle
Taraxacum officinale dandelion
Tussilago farfara coltsfoot
Urtica dioica stinging nettle

Certain plants, native and foreign, so forget their manners when introduced into the garden as to try to take over everywhere. Some need cultivated soil to do this and can be contained in the wild garden where the soil is little moved. Others succeed in the roughest areas. The beautifully scented, pale lavender heads of winter heliotrope, *Petasites fragrans*, appearing shortly after the new year, could tempt one to try it, but the delicate flowers give no hint of its territorial lust. Introduced in 1806 as a garden plant, it now covers roadside verges and other spots with huge tough leaves above rampaging stoloniferous roots.

Bluebells can be naturalized in grass beneath trees, but are invasive

Some bulbs can be a nuisance in cultivated areas. The bluebells, *Hyacinthoides non-scripta* and *H. hispanica*, the leafy grape hyacinth, *Muscari neglectum*, the star of Bethlehem, *Ornithogalum umbellatum*, and sometimes the green and white large *O. nutans* can increase at an alarming rate and smother choicer things. Some of the sorrels, *Oxalis* species, are ridiculously prolific too.

Other plants – mainly introduced and naturalized – that can be invasive and may have to be carefully controlled, even in the wild garden, include *Allium moly*, *A. triquetrum* and the native ramsons, *A. ursinum*; creeping bellflower, *Campanula rapunculoides*; yellow fumitory, *Corydalis lutea*; ivy-leaved toadflax, *Cymbalaria muralis*; and feverfew, *Tanacetum parthenium*.

Any site with very dominant weeds needs cleaning up before attempting a wild flower garden. Coarse couch grass and other strongly stoloniferous species should be eliminated throughout the area and preferably for some distance beyond to stop rapid recolonization from the edges.

Dealing with growing weeds is relatively easy, by either digging and hoeing them out, using a chemical weedkiller, or smothering them. Even really tough weeds will succumb to smothering and three of the growing months under secure black polythene should leave a weed-free blank canvas. Chemical warfare is quicker, although there will be a reservoir of weed seeds waiting for an opportunity to recolonize. If you have the patience to let a few crops of weeds germinate and to kill them at intervals, the store of seed is reduced and much later work can be avoided. Glyphosate is efficient and kills nearly all green plant life, but is harmless in the soil. Alloxydim-sodium is good for killing awkward grasses, including couch, though not annual meadow grass, but does not affect broad-leaved plants. (See also the Wisley handbook, *Weed control in the garden*.)

Once the desired mixture of wild flowers is growing, there is not likely to be a great problem with weeds. The natural ground cover will help to suppress them and the fact that the soil is left undisturbed will not provide the conditions to encourage them.

PROPAGATING WILD PLANTS

There is no difference in principle between increasing wild and cultivated plants. Herbaceous kinds like ox-eye daisy, *Leucanthemum vulgare*, can be divided in early autumn or spring in the normal way, using a spade, or forks back to back, to separate a clump into several parts. The older bits are discarded.

Several plants, such as violas, honeysuckle and heathers, can be increased by cuttings. Many may be layered in the spring or early summer and then severed, lifted and replanted in the autumn or following spring.

Seed is the most obvious method of propagation and is normally sown in spring or autumn. Here I would advise caution: just scattering the seeds where the plants are required may be fine for a large area of prepared soil or when one has an abundance of seeds, but if you are relying on bought packets, you will find relatively few seeds in some. It is wiser to sow the seeds in pots or trays, to prick out seedlings into modules or pots and then to plant out young, but strong, established plants.

The same applies to seeds collected in the wild, which must be ripe when gathered and are best sown immediately in a labelled pot or container. A podful of seed taken from the wild will not endanger a widespread species, but seed should never be collected from rare plants or from plants rare in a particular locality. (See also the Index, p. 61, for propagation methods).

13

mesh or strands of cotton stretched across. Annual weeds like groundsel and chickweed should be removed by hand, to allow the seedlings to have full benefit of the site. Some thinning may be necessary, but many of the cornfield weeds and other annuals can be left in clumps, where they will grow to look like individual plants and support each other when young. Finally, as the new community begins to get established, groups of plants raised in pots or trays can be planted.

If only a very small portion of lawn is to be used for a few wild flowers, you can dodge the full-scale operation outlined above. Instead, proceed by energetically raking the site, reducing the population of grasses dramatically, and then introduce the wild flowers – cowslips, primroses and fritillaries, for example – as established plants, or rake the seeds into the loose soil.

MOWING AND MAINTENANCE

My own plan is to designate parts of the meadow where the interest will be mainly in spring and others that take over in high summer and later. Where spring flowers predominate, the herbage is mown in early summer, while the other areas are left until autumn.

With the end of autumn, the meadow will be ready for a comprehensive tidy up. Patches may have been mown at different times through the year, but now much of the annual growth should be cleared away and mown short. Before this is done, there may be some plants that you wish to lift and divide. This is normally best carried out in the autumn, though if plants are to remain until the early spring, they need to be clearly labelled. Any plants that are overplaying their welcome should be restricted at this time, before mowing. Afterwards, it is more difficult to see the plants and their rootstocks.

A few plants can be left to hold the fort over the winter and provide contrast – umbelliferous plants like cow parsley, for instance, whose bleached stems may be allowed at least for the first half of the winter, or the wild teasel, *Dipsacus fullonum*. Odd clumps of grasses that remain attractive in winter can wait till the spring for their annual grooming, as can rushes and sedges.

In late winter, the grass-cutter gives a haircut before small bulbous plants or other early things have achieved sufficient height to fall under the blades.

With a scythe, sickle or power strimmer, incursions can be made when and where appropriate, to cut down grasses and plants that have passed their fruiting stage or are threatening others which

Common buttercups and daisies do well in grass

you wish to encourage. The gardener acts the part of nibbling sheep or cattle, preserving the low turf plants.

GRASSES

Grasses form the background to the meadow community. A good mixture would consist of sheep's fescue, *Festuca ovina*, the bent grasses, *Agrostis* species, and crested dog's tail, *Cynosurus cristatus*. These are the smaller kinds of grasses that predominate in chalk downlands and are capable of making a living on shallow poor soils. Grass introduced for farm animals and inherited by gardens is not suitable. Yorkshire fog, *Holcus lanatus*, which is a lawn weed, can be pretty, with pinkish seedheads turning more purple with maturity and ending silvery. The range of wild grasses is huge and adding some of the attractive smaller kinds will make the patchwork of the area much more interesting.

SPRING-FLOWERING PLANTS

Spring is probably the most effective season in the wild garden. From the winter, there may well be a few plants showing early blooms and, in sheltered spots, it is not uncommon to pick an odd wild primrose at Christmas. In mild winters, they can be blooming freely in the first three or even four months of the year. Violets too will respond to early mild weather by producing precocious blooms.

Lady's smock, *Cardamine pratensis*, flowers from April onwards

They grow happily where strong grasses do not suffocate them. *Viola riviniana*, the common dog violet (see p. 52), is the most widespread species, the scentless mauve-violet flowers being paler than those of the sweet violet, *V. odorata*. Pure albinos are frequent.

Common flowers such as daisies, buttercups and dandelions look well, but while the first can be kept within bounds quite easily, the seedling potential of dandelions is dangerous. Viewed dispassionately, dandelions can be magnificent, especially in association with groups of fritillaries – a pattern of gold with purple-mauves and whites. Blooming at the same time in moist grass, lady's smock or cuckoo flower, *Cardamine pratensis*, is lovely in a drift, with masses of flowers ranging from white through pale lilacs to deeper shades.

An easily managed favourite, the cowslip, *Primula veris*, has early leaves pressed to the ground, so that a mower may be taken over them without risk before the flower stems appear. Once established, seed is distributed and flourishing colonies quickly develop. Purists will keep the wild cowslip clear of coloured cultivated primroses and polyanthus, but sometimes, even in the best regulated gardens, accidents occur. The resulting coloured hybrids can be very pretty. The oxlip, *P. elatior*, stands midway between the cowslip and the primrose and is a worthy meadow plant.

Winter's end is marked by the snowdrops opening, the double form of the common snowdrop, *Galanthus nivalis* 'Flore Pleno', appearing several days before the single. Snowdrops are now so much part of the landscape that it is hard to believe they were probably introduced originally. They do well in grass, although they increase more quickly in a shrubbery or in light woodland.

The bulbous theme is continued by the wild daffodil, *Narcissus pseudonarcissus*, with perhaps companion clumps of the brighter all-yellow Tenby daffodil, *N. obvallaris*. The wild wood anemone, *Anemone nemorosa*, is a creeping rhizomatous plant, best in light woodland conditions, but happy in grass. It starts blooming with the wild daffodils. Its charming divided leaves and nodding blooms make one of the most engaging of spring pictures. The usual flowers of white flushed mauvy pink can be accompanied by selected clones that have pure white, all pink, or pale blue blooms. Soon after the petals have dropped, the plant seems to disappear and may have retreated below ground by the time the wild bluebell, *Hyacinthoides non-scripta*, opens its arched flowerheads. These seem more natural than those of the introduced Spanish bluebell, *H. hispanica*, with bolder erect spikes, and larger, more open bells. Related genera can be researched for others, such as the rare native *Scilla verna*, but this is not an easy plant and small species like the Mediterranean *S. bifolia* may be more amenable and easier to obtain from nurseries.

Wood anemone, *Anemone nemorosa*, is widespread in woodland and hedgerows throughout Britain

The snake's head fritillary, *Fritillaria meleagris*, and one or two wild tulips take the spring flush into May and June. *Tulipa sylvestris*, which appears in most British floras as a rare native plant but is in fact from the Continent, has weak stems carrying yellow flowers with green and red shading on the reverses. Some clones are more floriferous than others. Though also not a native, *T. sprengeri* from Asia Minor is a fine naturalizing plant, capable of seeding itself widely. It blooms late, in May and June – probably the last of all the tulips – and is a much larger plant, with more erect, 1 ft (30 cm) high stems topped by rusty red flowers that open widely. Both tulips are best in well drained soils. *Fritillaria meleagris* belongs in water meadows and will thrive in moister spots, though it does well in most soils. The large nodding heads of purple, mauve or creamy white may be more or less chequered and it sets abundant seed which, if gathered and sown, will quickly provide lots of new bulbs (see p. 14).

PLANTS FOR SUMMER AND AUTUMN EFFECT

Everyone will have their own sign of the beginning of summer. For me, it comes with the ox-eye daisies, *Leucanthemum vulgare*, crowding the road verges and meadows. Where there is broken

Ox-eye daisies and poppies are often found growing together in the wild and make an attractive combination

Common toadflax, *Linaria vulgaris*, grows in fields and hedge banks

soil, there are likely to be field poppies, *Papaver rhoeas*, growing and flowering. These used to stain the cornfields orange-red before selective weedkillers kept them all at bay. There is an army waiting to spring from the earth, for each pod can hold at least 3,000 seeds, which will remain viable for up to 80 years and germinate if the soil is disturbed. Small patches of broken soil will also serve for a few seeds of the very attractive toadflax, *Linaria vulgaris*, with spires of creamy gold, small, snapdragon flowers, reaching maybe only 9 in. (22 cm), but capable of 30 in. (75 cm).

Few plants looks so enchanting in light grass as *Viola tricolor* and *V. lutea*. The first is the wild pansy or heartsease and the flowers,

Mountain pansy, *Viola lutea*, inhabits grassland in hilly districts

while basically violet-purple, usually have greater or lesser amounts of white and yellow, all prettily veined. *Viola lutea* is found more often on higher ground and, despite its name, there are purple as well as very bright yellow forms. It grows better on grassy banks than in a border – a place where the leafier *V. tricolor* can have a party, making large plants with lots of flowers.

Moist soils
A later chapter (p. 43) describes many plants which enjoy wet conditions. Here, we can consider a few of those that grow well in moist grass. Rushes like the soft rush, *Juncus effusus*, and the

jointed rush, *J. articulatus*, may appear naturally, especially in acid soils. Similar in effect but unrelated are the sedges – a large genus of which there are around 80 native species, some very decorative (see also p. 43). The common sedge, *Carex nigra*, with dark flowering heads, indicates wet, often acid soils. The long-stalked yellow sedge, *Carex lepidocarpa*, has interesting flowering stems, with several nobbly spiky female ones below the topmost male.

More obviously ornamental are flowering plants. The devil's bit scabious, *Succisa pratensis*, has tight heads of flowers crowded together on the top of long stems and, unlike other scabiouses, lacks a ring of larger florets. The colour is violet-mauve, though white forms can be found. Common valerian, *Valeriana officinalis*, has nothing to do with the red valerian, *Centranthus ruber*, an introduced plant which delights in colonizing old walls, rocks and cliffs. The common valerian is not all that common now, usually inhabiting moist verges and wasteland. There, it can form thick colonies of very erect, strong growth, with pinnate leaves and tight umbels of small, pinkish white flowers. It will often stand 3–4 ft (90–120 cm) tall when flowering from June through to August.

Brooklime, *Veronica beccabunga*, is a more succulent plant than the common speedwell, *V. officinalis*. Leaves are broader and stems fatter, while the flowers, in long pointed spikes, are bright blue and generally produced from May until September. It is a low scrambler, growing in and out of water. The meadow crane's bill, *Geranium pratense*, has the typical divided foliage of wild geraniums, with large blooms of blue or pale purple held on stems that can reach 12–30 in. (30–75 cm). The square-stemmed St John's wort, *Hypericum tetrapterum*, grows very uprightly, 1 ft (30 cm) or up to nearly 3 ft (90 cm) high, with oval pointed leaves and glowing umbels of golden flowers.

Dry soils

Many plants are happy in well drained, dryish soils, even poor ones. Dry grass is just the place to have the common centaury, *Centaurium erythraea*. Depending on the food supply, the small plant may rest content with a single stem with a solitary bloom, but

Above: meadow crane's bill, *Geranium pratense*, blooms from June to September
Below: field scabious, *Knautia arvensis*, flourishes in dry chalky pastures and verges

usually it will produce several upright stems, from a few inches to almost 1 ft (30 cm) high, bearing many-headed sprays of five-petalled pink stars – making it one of the prettiest of all natives.

Owing to its creeping stems, the silverweed, *Potentilla anserina*, is a very dangerous colonizer in awkward spots, in the rock garden or on paths. On a sunny bank, it is all delight; the shining silvered leaves of seven or more pairs of serrated leaflets are handsome enough alone, but it spends gold freely and is rarely without flattish buttercup blossoms from May till the summer's end.

A number of wild orchids grow in chalkland grass. Many are listed among the 93 plants given special legal protection under the Wildlife and Countryside Act of 1981 (see p. 57). If they appear in your patch, as they can by seeds finding conditions to their liking, you should give thanks and encourage them. Orchids must not be taken from the wild, except if they are falling in front of a developer's bulldozer, in which case a local conservation or similar society should be alerted to resite them. The plants should be lifted with a substantial sod of turf around each one, as they resent disturbance and depend on certain micro-organisms present in the soil. Those on sale are usually collected abroad, often illegally – a trade that must be thoroughly condemned.

Some ordinary dry-area plants are worth growing. One is the pinky purple-flowered *Centaurea nigra* or lesser knapweed. It is a distinctive plant, while the greater knapweed, *C. scabiosa*, is altogether larger. The field scabious, *Knautia arvensis*, is probably the showiest of a number of related plants. Its mauve-blue wide flowers are made up of a pin-cushion of many florets, surrounded by a ring of larger ones, but with not a lot of foliage (see p. 25). Even more parsimonious with leaves is the harebell, *Campanula rotundifolia*, though it is generous with its blue flowers. Viper's bugloss, *Echium vulgare*, is seen most often in dry grasslands near the sea. It can be in bloom at any time throughout the summer and is a bold plant with very rough, hairy stems and leaves. The spikes of blue flowers shaded pink reach 1–3 ft (30–90 cm) high.

The beautiful bird's foot trefoil, *Lotus corniculatus*, has masses of gold and orange-flushed flowers, suggesting one of many popular names – eggs and bacon – and its leguminous nature is clearly stamped on miniature pea-like foliage and flowers. The flowering

---

Above: bird's foot trefoil, *Lotus corniculatus*, blooms from midsummer to early autumn
Below: the biennial viper's bugloss, *Echium vulgare*, is popular with insects

period is prolonged and overlaps that of other plants, like the field mouse-ear, *Cerastium arvense*, whose delicate stems and narrow foliage lean against neighbouring grasses and plants to hold their pure white blossom aloft. The common stork's bill, *Erodium cicutarium*, has finely cut, ferny foliage and a succession of small, bright pink flowers, which open in the morning and get on with their work of being pollinated so quickly that all may be complete by midday, when the petals can be dropped. Lady's bedstraw, *Galium verum*, produces quantities of tiny mustard-coloured flowers in many rounded heads.

Once every meadow was populated by a mixture of vetches. They are a handsome and interesting lot. The restharrow, *Ononis repens*, is a low spreading plant, with the leaves gently serrated and somewhat hairy and has large, rich reddish pink, pea flowers. Like many of the vetches and their relatives, it is found more on chalk and limestone soils, but is easy in all soils except very acid ones.

Attractive yellow-flowered leguminous plants include spotted medick, *Medicago arabica*, notable for its shamrock leaves with their central dark blotches; the commoner black medick, *M. lupulina*; and the tall melilot, *Melilotus altissima*, which was brought into Britain in the 1500s and is now seen in wasteland, roadsides and woods, as well as in grass. It makes a very fine, bushy plant, 2–4 ft (60–120 cm) high, with many spikes of mid-yellow flowers.

Lucerne, *Medicago sativa*, has had periods of popularity as a fodder crop and can be raided for garnishing salad and called by its other name – alfalfa. It is an upright strong plant 1–3 ft (30–90 cm) high, with attractive tripartite foliage gently serrated and neat conical flower spikes of violet-purple. Yellow variants are known.

Sprawling mats of horseshoe vetch, *Hippocrepis comosa*, create a profusion of rich golden flowers, often with red stripes or flushes. It is rather like the bird's foot trefoil, but is distinguished by the greater number of leaflets. The kidney vetch, *Anthyllis vulneraria*, has many tight bunches of flowers, again of similar colour. The zigzagging prostrate stems of the milk vetch, *Astragalus glycyphyllos*, bear clean-cut leaves of many pairs of widely oval leaflets and pale greenish cream-yellow flowers – pleasant but not dramatic.

A casual glance might dismiss the purple milk vetch, *Astragalus danicus*, as clover, but the intricate leaves of many small paired leaflets and the pinky purple flowers will reveal the difference. The non-native goat's rue, *Galega officinalis*, is an energetic leafy plant, with many leaflets and pretty spikes of lilac flowers, though white forms are frequent. With sticks or bushes to scramble over, it can get head high. It enjoys a moist spot.

Sanfoin, *Onobrychis viciifolia*, is another alien, with many tight oval spikes of reddish pink flowers, often purple-veined. It can range from a scrambling, almost prostrate plant to one capable of reaching nearly 3 ft (90 cm) high. Bush vetch, *Vicia sepium*, also trails around the ground, but it has tendrils to help it clamber upwards. Attractive many-paired foliage and one-sided tight sprays of pinky mauve flowers make this a pleasant plant, but it can be a weed in the garden border. The tufted vetch, *V. cracca*, is a tendrilled scrambling plant, with long, crowded, one-sided spikes of purplish blue flowers. Towards the end of the summer, it can be impressive; with support, the branched tendrils will help it to get up as far as 6–7 ft (2 m), but in grass it may be only 2 ft (60 cm) high.

There are many outstanding plants found most frequently on dry soils which are alkaline. These include the dyer's greenweed, *Genista tinctoria*, with masses of rich golden blossom, often at its best towards the end of the summer and devoid of spiny armour. Another yellow-flowered member of a subshrubby genus, the perforate St John's wort, *Hypericum perforatum*, is a very pretty little weed of grass, hedgesides and open woodland. With short, slender, lateral branches and neat small leaves, it has upright stems topped by a spray of small, bright yellow flowers, unusually pencilled or dotted black on the petal edges.

Chicory, *Cichorium intybus*, can be dramatic, 1–4 ft (30–120 cm) high, with branching stems carrying many large, brilliant blue flowers. It has a long flowering season from midsummer until late autumn. The flowers open with the sun and are best in the morning; in dull weather they tend to stay closed. Bugloss, *Anchusa arvensis*, is another bold plant, with rough hairy leaves and stems. It grows to about 2 ft (60 cm) and produces wide heads of shining blue flowers, as bright as the brightest forget-me-not.

Other chalkland kinds worth trying are the field gentian, *Gentianella campestris*, which has subdued purple flowers in tightish upward-facing bunches, each flower being long-tubed and four-petalled; the small scabious, *Scabiosa columbaria*, a meagrely leaved plant, with long stems and tight button flowerheads of bluish lilac, which act as service stations for many insects; and the eyebright, *Euphrasia nemorosa*, an annual and member of the Scrophulariaceae family with their intricate, unusually shaped flowers. The hooded tops and lower jutting lips in three sections, each bi-lobed, make one think of little orchids, especially as the white flowers are delicately marked with purple lines and shading, plus a honey-golden blotch. It can be anything up to a foot (30 cm) high.

Hedgerows, Shrubberies and Banks

HEDGES AND SCREENS

Many native plants, remnants of a woodland flora, are making their last ditch stand by country hedgerows. Some are in the ditches. The hedgerows are important habitats, but garden hedges of privet and Leyland cypress are very bad news for wild species, as virtually nothing grows beneath these greedy plants.

Old farm hedges may contain many species; new ones are likely to be dominated by hawthorn, *Crataegus monogyna* (see p. 4). If you inherit an old farm hedge, do not rush to replace it with something more domestic. The old one will be more interesting than immaculately groomed *leylandii*, will support much more insect and bird life and may already have a considerable population of plants both in and below it, which you can add to. Perhaps one or two trees may need to be removed: elder, for instance, is better in the wild.

If you have to plant a new hedge, it is ecological sense to use a mixture of species. A barrier or informal screen may be even better than a hedge and will save many hours of trimming, although plants which will be allowed a chance to show their character need some initial training and restraint. Young plants should be encouraged to break into several growths low down to make an effective barrier and each winter a number of strong growths may have to be cut back. The choice of species for hedges and screens depends mainly on the space available. In small gardens, it is wise to avoid the stronger kinds, like hawthorns and sprawling dog roses, and to go for foreign species such as smaller berberises, cotoneasters and less rampant roses. Native hedge plants include:

Acer campestre field maple
Carpinus betulus hornbeam
Cornus sanguinea dogwood
Corylus avellana hazel
Crataegus laevigata Midland thorn
C. monogyna hawthorn
Euonymus europaeus spindleberry

Fagus sylvatica beech
Ilex aquifolium holly
Prunus spinosa blackthorn
Rhamnus cathartica buckthorn
Rosa canina dog rose
Viburnum lanata wayfaring tree
V. opulus guelder rose

The dog rose, *Rosa canina*, is a familiar sight in our hedgerows

Honeysuckle, *Lonicera periclymenum*, a beautiful climber for the garden

CLIMBING PLANTS

Plants like honeysuckles are obvious climbers, others just welcome support. All can adorn a hedge. Good forms of *Lonicera periclymenum* are sold as garden plants. The strong-growing old man's beard, *Clematis vitalba*, may be foresworn in areas where it festoons every farm hedge, but elsewhere it can be introduced and enjoyed for its cream-green flowers and silken seedheads. The twining stems of the hop, *Humulus lupulus*, grow each year from perennial rootstocks, race up any support and produce handsome autumn seedheads. The golden-leaved form, 'Aureus', is the one usually grown in gardens.

Black bryony, *Tamus communis*, with lacquered heart-shaped leaves and autumn stems garlanded with shining, gold and scarlet beads, looks magnificent, but the fruit is poisonous. Woody nightshade, *Solanum dulcamara*, is another highly decorative, quick-growing, clambering species, its violet purple and yellow flowers followed by green oval fruits, which turn first yellow and then red. Like all parts of the plant, these are toxic, but not to the lethal degree of the black-berried deadly nightshade.

Yellow flag, *Iris pseudacorus*, at the edge of a pond

MOIST HEDGESIDE AND DITCH

A hedge and ditch give the partial shade, coolness and moisture that many plants enjoy. Sedges, rushes and plants like the yellow flag, *Iris pseudacorus*, and the meadowsweet, *Filipendula ulmaria*, will revel in such a site. The buttercup family too comes into its own. The marsh marigold, *Caltha palustris*, is one of the most outstanding spring flowers (see p. 42) and the double form a treasured garden plant. The spendthrift gold of the lesser celandine, *Ranunculus ficaria*, with its marbled heart-shaped leaves, is also a joy early in the year in a wild place. In the garden, however, it is an exasperating weed, with the easily broken, little tubers instigating fresh plants. There are selected forms with white or orange flowers and some with the stained outer petals even more dramatically dark. Other buttercup relatives may make an appearance. The lesser spearwort, *R. flammula*, with typical buttercup flowers and narrow spear-shaped leaves, reaches as high as 1–2 ft (30–60 cm) in conducive spots.

Globe flowers in the garden are usually forms of *Trollius chinensis*. The native *T. europaeus* is less brassy than most of these foreign hybrids, having pleasant divided foliage and plenty of large, limy yellow flowers, with the petals wrapped over to give a globe effect. It is tidy and erect, reaching 1–2 ft (30–60 cm). This is certainly a plant to include – easy without being badly invasive, attractive in its foliage at all times and free with its long-lasting flowers from June to August.

The umbelliferous horde includes cow parsley and hogweed, but wild angelica, *Angelica sylvestris*, has an extra touch of class. Its pinnate foliage is impressive, the stems bold and the crowded white flowerheads in late summer more disciplined than some of its relatives. Another of this brood worth considering is sweet cicely, *Myrrhis odorata*, flowering in May and June – a plant still used in the kitchen and known for the aniseed smell when any part is bruised. Although introduced, it is one of the more frequent roadside plants of northern Britain. The foliage is fern-like and, atop the strong stalk, small white flowers are clasped close by the many incurving stems.

Arum maculatum has lots of English names, of which cuckoo-pint and lords and ladies are the most used. There are forms in which the large arrow-shaped leaves are variegated; all are highly polished and can be more or less marked with purple. In April and May, a pale flowering spathe surrounds the upright, brown, poker-like spadix – the preacher in the pulpit. Tight bunches of red berries follow and look handsome, but are very poisonous (see p. 36).

Some daisies enjoy damp positions. Fleabane, *Pulicaria dysenterica*, has wide disc flowers with short yellow petals, appearing in August. It may accompany the Welsh poppy *Meconopsis cambrica*, with yellow flowers opening through the summer and seeding all over. This grows in a variety of sites, from woodland and hedgerows to damp walls, where it may meet the hart's tongue fern (p. 41), herb robert (p. 37), and the yellow and orange toadflax. Purple loosestrife, *Lythrum salicaria*, is spectacular, especially beside wet ditches, with many tight, narrow, long spikes of rich purple-red or pinky crimson held erect in late summer to autumn (see p. 46).

HEDGESIDE AND SHRUBBERY

Wild hedge and shrubbery that has been redefined as an environmental centre will support a wide variety of plants (see also p. 39). The more civilized shrubbery area will suit the unusual evergreen shrub, *Ruscus aculeatus*, or butcher's broom, together with the foxglove, *Digitalis purpurea*, lily of the valley, *Convallaria majalis*, snowdrops, and Solomon's seal, *Polygonatum multiflorum*, bearing clusters of white bells in late spring. To these we can add the red campion, *Silene dioica*, strikingly beautiful when the bright pink flowers open in early summer, and the yellow archangel, *Lamiastrum galeobdolon*, one of the more obviously attractive of the dead nettles. Space can be allowed for a plant or two of white dead nettle, *Lamium album*. Other relatives include the maroon-flowered, long-spiked *Stachys sylvatica*, or hedge woundwort, and the rather similar but clean-shaven betony, *S. officinalis*.

Common mallow, *Malva sylvestris*, is impressive in the wild, perhaps over 3 ft (90 cm) tall, with mauvy pink flowers in summer (see p. 36). Far more refined and better in the garden is the purer pink-flowered, *M. moschata*, only half as high. Basal leaves are more or less rounded, but up the stems they become more and more divided and fern-like. There is a very attractive, silky, pure white form. It would look well by some of the geranium species, such as *Geranium pyrenaicum*, with lilac-pink flowers.

There are several plants that lean on shrubs for support. Greater stitchwort, *Stellaria holostea*, is one of the loveliest, winking open vividly white flowers in late spring. Delicately stemmed and with narrow pointed leaves, it is a plant of character, dancing up the hedge, not lolling on it like a drunkard. Lesser stitchwort, *S. graminea*, has even narrower leaves and petals. More obviously a climber is the narrow-leaved everlasting pea, *Lathyrus sylvestris*, with lots of tendrils and an abundance of rich pink, red, small, pea flowers on neat stems from June to August. *Lathyrus latifolius* is the foreigner, with larger flowers. *Corydalis claviculata* is a discreet delicate-looking climber equipped with branched tendrils from the leaf ends and making airy passes upwards, with pretty little leaves and clusters of creamy white, tubular flowers. It has the manners and appearance of a pea or vetch relative, but is more closely related to the poppies and brassicas.

Some of the lovely plants of woodland are dangerously extrovert. One is put on guard about galiums when realizing that cleavers or goosegrass, a pestilential weed, is one of their number. Lady's bedstraw, *Galium verum* (p. 28), is very pretty in hedge or grass, but should be barred from more civilized areas. Sweet woodruff, *G. odoratum*, is a little more circumspect, but an eye needs to be kept on it. Erect stems 6–12 in. (15–30 cm) high are neatly dressed in small whorls of leaves and topped with sprays of tiny white flowers in early summer. More showy and a plant that often appears in our gardens is the woodland spurge, *Euphorbia amygdaloides*, a subshrub with long oval leaves of bluey green, often suffused with purple, and flowerheads pleasantly contrasted in limy yellow.

Stinking hellebore, *Helleborus foetidus*, is a popular plant, acting

an evergreen part with masses of dark palmate foliage and producing fountains of pale green flowers in winter and spring. *Helleborus viridis*, in habit close to the Lenten roses, has large, wide, vividly green flowers.

BANKS

Perhaps you know 'a bank whereon the wild thyme blows, where oxlips and the nodding violet grows'. These would be *Thymus praecox*, with *Primula elatior* and the dog violets, *Viola canina* and *V. riviniana* (pp. 19, 52). Maybe the little pansy, *V. tricolor*, peeps wide-eyed through the grass and, in well drained spots, the bright yellow *V. lutea* (p. 23) might smile.

Wood sorrel, *Oxalis acetosella*, busies itself burrowing below the surface and poking up shamrock leaves and white flowers throughout the summer. Wild marjoram, *Origanum vulgare*, with neat foliage and posies of pale pink flowers, is found on drier chalky banks, but will manage well enough in most soils. Feverfew, *Tanacetum parthenium*, impresses with its masses of white and yellow daisy flowers, but needs controlling, while tansy, *T. vulgare*, makes points with rich green, velvety, divided foliage and heads of yellow flowers without wide outer florets.

Vetches may be found on the bank – some that have been mentioned already (p. 28) and also perhaps the bitter vetch, *Lathyrus montanus*, with its crimson pea flowers fading to blue, and the delightful meadow vetchling, *L. pratensis*, having bright yellow flower bunches held neatly above recumbent stems.

Other wildlings like agrimony, *Agrimonia eupatoria*, with its narrow spikes of yellow flowers and burred fruits, may be given a foothold – but just a foothold. We might allow herb robert, *Geranium robertianum*, one of the prettiest of weeds. Its divided leaves and stems flushed red are beautiful even without the usual shower of little pink flowers. It quickly colonizes uncovered soils and will manage well enough on crumbling walls and waste spots. It should be culled where it threatens to engulf other plants less well able to look after themselves.

Above: *Arum maculatum* (*left*), supplies interest with leaves, flowering spathes and berries; wood sorrel, *Oxalis acetosella* (*right*), is very tolerant of shade
Below: common mallow, *Malva sylvestris* (*left*), is attractive to bees; wild thyme (*right*) is less aromatic than garden thyme

Beds and Borders

In the garden, many wild plants are happier in organized natural communities, but some are equally good in a normal herbaceous border or mixed island bed. By using several native shrubs or even trees, a bed devoted to wild plants can be kept attractive at all times. Spring and summer may be more flowery, but in autumn and winter barks, stem silhouettes, flowers, berries and other fruits, evergreen foliage, seedheads, as well as the bleached stems and leaves of grasses, ferns and umbelliferous plants, all add interest.

TREES AND SHRUBS

The bones of the design can be made by planting trees and shrubs such as the following:

Acer campestre field maple
Betula pendula silver birch
Calluna vulgaris ling
Daphne laureola spurge laurel
D. mezereum mezereon
Erica cinerea bell heather
E. tetralix cross-leaved heath
E. vagans Cornish heath
Euonymus europaeus spindleberry
Genista pilosa hairy greenweed
Hippophae rhamnoides sea buckthorn

Ilex aquifolium holly
Juniperus communis juniper
Myrica gale bog myrtle
Ruscus aculeatus butcher's broom
Salix lanata woolly willow (see also p. 49)
S. repens creeping willow
Sorbus aria whitebeam
S. aucuparia rowan
Ulex europaeus gorse

Winter doubles the value of evergreens such as butcher's broom, gorse – especially the double-flowered form, *Ulex europaeus* 'Flore Pleno' – and spurge laurel. The herbaceous *Helleborus foetidus* (p. 35) is evergreen and deserves consideration in planting plans.

Silver birches are attractive in the winter, but are greedy surface-rooting trees. With them can be planted their natural neighbours, the heathers, gorses and brooms. Other acid-loving plants might also be used, such as the vacciniums – *Vaccinium myrtillus*, *V. vitis-idaea* and *V. oxycoccos*. Some hypericums look shrubby, even if they grow afresh each year from a perennial rootstock. *Hypericum perforatum* (p. 29) and *H. tetrapterum* (p. 24) are both neat erect plants and not out of place in civilization.

Spindleberry, *Euonymus europaeus*, a native shrub or small tree found particularly on chalky soil

BULBS, PERENNIALS AND ANNUALS

Groups of bulbs can be planted among the shrubs – wild daffodils, bluebells, snowdrops, *Tulipa sylvestris*, star of Bethlehem, *Ornithogalum umbellatum*, and snake's head fritillaries (pp. 14, 21), together with the summer snowflake, *Leucojum aestivum*, and autumn crocus, *Colchicum autumnale*. Primroses, cowslips, violets, lady's smock (p. 19) and marsh marigold (pp. 33, 42) will give more flower and wax large in borders without the competition of the wild. However, fertilizers are banned, as there is a danger of plants outgrowing their natural character. It is unwise to use such prolific increasers as lesser celandine (p. 33), some of the pretty speedwells and later-blooming polygonums (p. 47).

The vetches (p. 28) should certainly be considered and, of other legumes, the bird's foot trefoil and tall melilot are two excellent kinds. Field poppies are colourful, but developing seed pods need watching. Toadflax (p. 22) is very attractive and chicory (pp. 1, 29) is highly decorative towards the end of the summer.

In beds with broken soil, it is possible to grow flowers formerly well known among arable crops, but now extinct or nearly so. The corn cockle, *Agrostemma githago*, is an annual best sown in the spring, having large, reddish purple flowers with sharp calyx segments pointing far beyond the petals. It was probably introduced in Roman times. Field cow wheat, *Melampyrum arvense*, is

The pretty corn cockle, *Agrostemma githago*, has become very uncommon among arable crops

another once widespread cornfield weed – a handsome upright plant, with crowded spikes of snapdragon flowers in purple-pink and yellow.

Some spurges enjoy cultivated soil. Annuals such as *Euphorbia helioscopia*, the sun spurge, look distinctive in their lime and golden livery, with the lime-gold bracts providing the colour, like saucers round the tiny flowers. It colonizes rapidly, broadcasting explosive seedpods all around. Some very attractive grasses such as the perennial quaking grass, *Briza media*, can be almost too successful in going forth and increasing, unless they are curbed by cutting off the flowering heads.

FERNS

There are many splendid native ferns which are too good to miss. They can be grown in beds, by hedgerows, in shrubberies or in awkward corners and smaller ones look well with rock plants.

Ferns found growing on walls include the wall rue, *Asplenium ruta-muraria*, with 1–2 in. (3–6 cm) dark fronds; the very pretty maidenhair spleenwort, *A. trichomanes*, with narrow long-pointed fronds of precise, paired, flat leaflets (pinnae); and the rusty-back fern, *A. ceterach*, a particularly endearing dwarf, with light green fronds of small rounded pinnae, the undersides covered with rusty brown scales.

The standard large male fern, *Dryopteris filix-mas*, may be too rampant, but it has many smaller interesting cultivars well worth collecting. The lady fern, *Athyrium filix-femina*, is rather more graceful and it too has lots of attractive forms. The broad buckler-fern *Dryopteris dilatata*, has more intricately cut, large fronds and, as it is more or less evergreen, it is an effective garden plant. The largest native is the royal fern, *Osmunda regalis*, capable of making 6–9 ft (2–3 m) across in midsummer. It turns fawn with the frost.

Possibly the most sought after of native ferns is the soft shield fern, *Polystichum setiferum*, an evergreen with rounded clumps of very neatly and intricately cut, long, triangular fronds, looking velvety smooth and especially lovely as the silky new ones unfurl in spring. There are many fine mutants.

For evergreen colour, the hart's tongue fern, *Asplenium scolopendrium*, is useful, growing easily in many places, but particularly good in moist shady spots. Its numerous, polished, undivided fronds glisten with health. There are unusual forms, 'Crispum' being particularly attractive, with the frond margins deckled like a ruff.

Wet and Watery Sites

Farming methods since the Second World War have led to the filling in of most of the small ponds that were once a feature of the countryside and much farmland has become well drained as a result of subsidies and encouragement to produce maximum yields. With the elimination of moister habitats and the use of weedkillers, many formerly widespread plants have become rare and some are lost. Now there is a movement to save the more unusual plant environments and manage some land for a wider variety of plant and animal life. However, many more wet sites are still needed for moisture-loving plants – often among our most distinctive flora.

Even a small garden has considerable variations in soil moisture. For instance, in a sheltered north-facing site, which gets neither the sun nor the wind that dries the soil surface elsewhere, it will be possible to grow plants found wild in much wetter conditions. Soil levels some inches or feet below the norm will be cooler and wetter and should suit those moisture-lovers which inhabit moist grassland and ditches (see pp. 23 and 33).

WETLAND GRASSES AND SEDGES

Very boggy ground is fine for some attractive sedges and wetland grasses. Usually growing in acid soils rich in peat, these will manage well enough in garden soils that are near neutral. The most widespread is the common spike-rush, *Eleocharis palustris*, a plant often appearing naturally on moist soil. Cylindrical, erect, dark stems reach 6–24 in. (15–60 cm) tall, with small tight flowering heads. The bottom of each spike is ensheathed by a brownish scale for a generous length. Common cottongrass, *Eriophorum angustifolium*, has three-sided stems growing 8–24 in. (20–60 cm) tall. The nodding heads become very noticeable after pollination, as the fine hairs round the ovary lengthen to make attractive silky balls, lasting many weeks in late summer and autumn.

Among the many sedges are such striking plants as the pendulous sedge, *Carex pendula*, with triangular sharp-edged stems and rough, yellowish green leaves about 1 in. (2.5 cm) across, tending to

Marsh marigold, *Caltha palustris*, is an obvious choice for a wet situation

arch over at a height of 2–3 ft (60–90 cm). The undersides of the leaves are a richer blue-green. The flowering stems can reach 4 ft (120 cm) or more; they start upright, but in maturity they bend to display long, hanging, narrow tassels as much as 6 in. (15 cm) long.

The true bulrush, *Schoenoplectus lacustris*, is a meagrely leaved plant of water and boggy ground, with rich green stems reaching 3–9 ft (90–270 cm) tall. The relatively small, brown flowerheads are held close or more loosely on fine stems. The reedmace, *Typha latifolia*, often mistakenly called bulrush, is the very large water plant with dark, upright, poker heads. It is too large for the average garden, but there are more manageable, smaller, foreign species in this genus.

PLANTS FOR WET SOILS

Comfrey, *Symphytum officinale*, is a large tough plant, with leafy upright stems 1–4 ft (30–120 cm) high and close bunches of well calyxed bells in purple, pink, cream or white. The tuberous comfrey, *S. tuberosum*, is shorter, 9–24 in. (22–60 cm), and more refined, with large oval leaves and long, bell-shaped, crowded, nodding flowers of yellow. This is commoner in the north, while the larger one is more widespread in the south of England.

Yellow loosestrife, *Lysimachia vulgaris* (not a relative of the purple loosestrife, p. 34), makes clumps of upright stems with spear-shaped leaves and clusters of bright golden five-petalled flowers in wide pyramids. In cultivation, it can stand 3–5 ft (90–150 cm) tall in the summer. Ragged robin, *Lychnis flos-cuculi*, is very distinctive but increasingly scarce. Lòw leafy stems work at photosynthesis, while tall slender ones reach up 2 ft (60 cm) or more, displaying bright pink flowers. Their petals are usually divided into four narrow fingers, with small, white, divided segments in the centre.

Lousewort is the unattractive name for the pretty *Pedicularis sylvatica*, which grows in marshy ground where moisture-loving liver-fluke and certain snails also live. It is a dwarf, with leaves divided into opposite pairs of lobes rather like the maidenhair spleenwort fern of old walls (p. 41). Rich pink or red flowers emerge from large inflated calyces, a tall hood overreaching the lower three-lobed spreading petal.

Ragged robin, *Lychnis flos-cuculi*, is visited by butterflies

The scabious clan spread their bets, some being restricted to dry ground, others, like devil's bit scabious (p. 24), to marshes and wet places. Here, a neighbour may be the marsh cinquefoil, *Potentilla palustris*. This unusual species likes wet and has serrated five-lobed leaves, with heads of dull reddish brown flowers, star-shaped from the longer pointed sepals backing the petals. Tidy-minded gardeners are wary of polygonums, as these energetic plants often go walkabout, producing quantitites of dock-like leaves. Bistort, *Polygonum bistorta*, can be one such, but a restricted colony looks well when topped by the many slender-stemmed tight poker-heads of pinky red flowers.

No need to fear prosecution for growing the hemp agrimony, *Eupatorium cannabinum*. It has medicinal properties, but it is not the drug plant. In lush spots, it reaches 3–4 ft (90–120 cm), to make handsome, large, upright plants, the stems well clothed with large, long, serrated leaves. These tend to arch away, the whole being topped by dense clusters of many small, pinky red flowers in packed, lightly domed panicles.

Growing with heathers in wet soils are the rare marsh gentian, *Gentiana pneumonanthe*, and the lovely grass of Parnassus, *Parnassia palustris*. The gentian is a threatened species, becoming rarer as boggy sites become smaller and fewer. It is small, with neat, narrow, polished leaves and unbranching upright stems of a few inches, maybe 1 ft (30 cm) in good conditions. These are topped with deep blue, long-tubed, typical gentian flowers, with the five petals turning outwards, several flowers being closely held in the axils of the top one or two leaves. Points of similarity between *Parnassia palustris* and grass are minimal. It is related to the saxifrages, but its leaves are heart-shaped and long-stalked rather like those of violets. Many slender stems reach up 6–12 in. (15–30 cm), with one tight-clasped stalkless leaf about a third of the way up and, at the top, a frank, open, shining white flower, like a pure-hearted, very fine, albino buttercup. Closer examination reveals delicate grey veining and a number of wide yellow staminodes – a showy adaptation of the normal stamens.

Purple loosestrife, *Lythrum salicaria*, grows in marshes and at the edge of lakes

47

— Rock Gardens and Raised Beds —

It could be an interesting challenge to furnish a rock garden with native alpine plants only. British populations of these plants are very small and must be protected, but all those mentioned here are available from nurseries and alpine specialists. No plant should be taken from the wild.

SHRUBS

Dwarf willows could form the background to a collection of small plants. The woolly willow, *Salix lanata*, is a fine shrub growing to about 2 ft (60 cm) high and wider. The leaves are broad ovals of silver-grey, in youth silky above and below. Male plants have relatively large, honey-gold, upright, rounded catkins, females have green ones. The very prostrate *S. reticulata* has tough, dark, round leaves attractively embossed with a pattern of veins – really a very classy plant. This grows on damp mountain ledges, while *S. lanata* will be found leaning over high mountain streams.

Betula nana is the dwarf birch of moorland. It varies in height up to 3 ft (90 cm) or even considerably more, but small neat forms are available. Heathers and related genera such as *Vaccinium* (p. 39), *Andromeda* and *Arctostaphylos* can provide low shrubby support. Totally unrelated and very attractive is the mountain avens, *Dryas octopetala*, a tough, scrambling, compact, prostrate shrub, with small oak leaves in dark polished green. The flowers, in June and July, are large, open and creamy white, showing its relationship to the roses, and are followed by decorative fluffy seedheads.

ALPINE PLANTS

From our higher hills come some plants that are quickly recognized by alpine enthusiasts. The saxifrages are a pretty little series, led by the very distinct *Saxifraga oppositifolia*, with low trailing stems of small dark leaves. It is gorgeous in spring, when relatively large, upward-staring, rich reddish purple bells often hide the rest of the

---

Above: mountain avens, *Dryas octopetala*, clinging to the top of a wall
Below: thrift, *Armeria maritima*, covers the cliffs of the British coastline

49

plant. The summer-flowering S. *aizoides* is found in the wetter mountain sites, but in the garden does not need water splashing near by. Rather fleshy foliage makes a bed of shining leaves, each about ½ in (1 cm) long, with stems above reaching 6 in. (15 cm), each with three to over a dozen yellow blooms. There are also pinky red forms.

Saxifraga granulata is a lowland plant of banksides and meadows, where it persists by means of tiny bulbs. Close sprays of white flowers reach 6–12 in. (15–30 cm) tall in late spring. Usually found in moist spots, sometimes in screes, but sometimes in drier, less rocky places, S. *hypnoides* makes dense tufts of polished little leaves – the more moisture present the more extensive the growth. Above the foliage almost leafless 3–6 in. (7–15 cm) stems carry sprays of good-sized white flowers in summer.

Some small drabas look like saxifrages, though they belong to the Cruciferae – on the whole an uninspiring family. Hoary whitlow grass, *Draba incana*, is a short-lived mountain plant, with a mass of small hairy leaves and, above these, many stiff stems each bearing several small white flowers in June and July. *Draba muralis* is a little annual, at its best on walls where it has a limited diet to keep it small and neat with tiny white flowers. More impressive is yellow whitlow grass, *D. aizoides*, the popular rock garden plant, which is a doubtful native. It has thick tufts of tight, dark green leaves and relatively large, rich yellow flowers held above them. Some forms are shorter-stemmed.

Other small plants, though not from mountains, are thought of as 'alpines'. The thrift, *Armeria maritima*, of our rocky coastline is pleasing, with rose-pink flowers throughout the summer (see p. 48). There are named forms, including a white one. The milkwort, *Polygala vulgaris*, grows in short grass, often in dry sites. It reaches only 2–4 in. (5–10 cm) high, with plain, dark, polished, longish, oval leaves and small, deep blue flowers, the petals peeping from the pair of blue enclosing sepals. It can be in bloom from spring until late autumn. The maiden pink, *Dianthus deltoides*, is a rarity found on dry banks and similar spots. A low mat of dark green leaves is topped with many slender stems of flat, fringed, pinky red flowers in late summer. Forms grown in the garden are often more richly coloured, the leaves becoming very dark. It comes easily from seed and so may be tried in grassy areas, as well as with rock garden plants. The Cheddar pink, *D. gratianopolitanus*, is a cliff-dweller, with low tufts of narrow grey-green leaves and blue-grey stems carrying bright, flat, fringed, rose-pink flowers of very reasonable size.

Some plants are almost more frequent in printed floras than in nature. The Snowdon lily, *Lloydia serotina*, is one – a real rarity which, in Britain, is found only in Snowdonia. It is a tiny bulbous relative of the tulips and has thin leaves 3–4 in. (7–10 cm) tall, the same height as the slender stem bearing the single, white, starry flower, with its longitudinal narrow purple veins. The alpine campion, *Lychnis alpina*, is compact, with tight heads of bright pink flowers, also produced in June. *Diapensia lapponica* is a tricky arctic plant in limited residence on one Scottish mountain.* It is a little 2 in. (5 cm) huddle of bright green leaves, more or less in whorls, just above which reach stems carrying white blossom seemingly borrowed from a saxifrage.

The much loved spring gentian, *Gentiana verna*, is a rare scattered plant of the higher ground where Yorkshire, Durham and Cumbria converge, but a more familiar plant of the Alps. Low compact rosettes of pale green leaves back the azure pigment of the distinctly five-petalled flowers – the vividest of deep blues. It seems to do as well in moist heavy soils as in well drained ones. The spring gentian may be partnered in bloom by the dainty bird's eye primrose, *Primula farinosa*. This pops up again, though sparingly, on some Scottish mountains and in northern England. The small, low-pressed, primula leaves are grey-green above and white below with the 'farina' or meal. Slender stems carry an open umbel of shining, bright pink flowers, yellow in their stamened centres. Only 3–4 in. (7–10 cm) tall in the wild, it may edge higher in the fleshpots of civilization. There is a Scottish version, *P. scotica*, an elfin only half the size with stubbier tiny leaves and blooms. Seed should be sown regularly of these primulas, so that one is not left bereft if older plants suddenly die.

The lovely pasque flower, *Pulsatilla vulgaris*, is a rarity of some dry grassy banks, mainly on chalk. English specimens vary from the normal rich violet to more claret-red shades and to lavender-greys close to white. The much divided, ferny, light green leaves are hairy, as are the stems and large flower buds. The open velvet blooms, in April and May, have a central boss of golden stamens. These do their job and fluffy seedheads follow. Plants should be only a few inches tall; rich soil can encourage a *nouveau riche* opulence.

*Now reported growing on one or two Scottish golf courses.

Wildlife in the Garden

BUTTERFLIES

Of approximately 50 species of British butterflies, about 20 are dependent on woodland habitats. Mixed woodlands are the most supportive, while conifer plantations are near-deserts. The host plants for larvae and adult butterflies are varied. Wild violets are important to at least four species – the high brown fritillary, the silver-washed fritillary, the pearl-bordered and the small pearl-bordered – which lay their eggs on violets and whose larvae feed on them. Wood whites feed heavily on leguminous plants like bird's foot trefoil, *Lotus corniculatus*, which is also on the calling list of the dingy skipper. Gorgeous purple emperors are very dependent on the sallow, *Salix caprea*, as foodstuff for the larvae and the adults spend their time in the canopy of oaks and beeches. Purple hairstreak larvae are brought up on oak leaves and adults are never far from these trees.

Gardens may mimic the glade and broken light of woodland rides, the preferred environment of many butterflies. Hedgerows can be useful too. White admirals wrap their eggs in honeysuckle leaves and brimstones look out for the buckthorn, *Rhamnus cathartica*. Drifts of stinging nettles are not normally highspots of a garden, but they are the staple feed of three of our loveliest butterflies – the peacocks, red admirals and small tortoiseshells that come in such welcome numbers to buddleias and michaelmas daisies.

Other garden plants attractive to butterflies include most daisies, single dahlias, alyssum, catmint, honesty, sweet william, valerian and the autumn-flowering heads of *Sedum spectabile*, where you will find the splendid red admirals and painted ladies. However, painted ladies lay their eggs on thistles. Marbled white, wall brown, gatekeeper, ringlet, meadow brown and speckled wood larvae manage on unmown grasses. Small coppers like docks. Orange tips are reared on hedge mustard and other cruciferous plants. Holly blues raise their first brood on holly and a second in late summer on the flower buds of ivy, the chrysalids then over-wintering.

Dog violet, *Viola riviniana*, prefers shady conditions in grass

BIRDS

Birds add such life to the garden that few would wish to exclude them, although they can be extremely irritating pests. Finches, particularly bullfinches, attack fruit flower buds; house sparrows reduce the first few primroses to shreds, going on to fell crocuses and to vandalize unprotected seed beds; wood pigeons raid brassicas and other plants, while magpies eat and kill other birds' eggs and nestlings; jays can be destructive too, but they eat lots of insects.

However, the balance between beneficial and harmful effects generally tilts in favour of the birds. Aphids are dispatched in wholesale numbers, caterpillars disappear down many different throats, eggs and chrysalids of less welcome insects are plucked and swallowed by robins, tits, hedge sparrows and seed-eating finches. Even the delinquent house sparrow takes a good toll of aphids and other harmful insects. Tits are likely to be the most beneficial birds, repaying our offering of winter food by destroying huge numbers of eggs, larvae and insects.

Making the garden more attractive to birds and wildlife generally may mean curbing some inclinations. Extreme tidiness is out, since fallen leaves encourage insects and entice toads, frogs, and other animals, together with many birds, to forage. Similarly, rotten wood may be full of insect life and will be regularly visited by birds. Most garden birds are happiest in light woodland or places where scrub offers refuge, food and nesting sites. Trees and shrubs will therefore make gardens much more bird-friendly. Water is also important, not only for thirsty birds but for its insect life.

Trees such as silver birch, hawthorn, alder and the aspen, *Populus tremula*, all have plenty of associated insect life and large trees like the oak support a whole eco-system within their branches and below. Berrying plants, such as holly, hawthorn, rowan, honeysuckle, berberis, cotoneaster and malus, attract blackbirds and other thrushes and possibly waxwings, redwings and fieldfares; the latter particularly enjoy juicy yew berries. Teasles, thistles, Compositae members and grasses attract insects and thereby birds, some of which will be equally interested in the seed. Most of the daisy family provide seeds for birds and it can be a mistake to clear away dead michaelmas daisies, sunflowers and rudbeckias. Seeding snapdragons and forget-me-nots may be visited by finches.

Campions and foxgloves at the edge of a rhododendron wood

Conservation and Endangered Species

We can try to maintain the present improverished state of our landscape and flora to prevent even further loss, or we can try to encourage the remaining species and replace some of those that were formerly abundant. The Nature Conservancy Council aims to protect our heritage, but it does not endorse the introduction of rare plants into the countryside. Indeed, the Council appears less than happy about gardeners growing them in gardens, fearing that such plants may escape into wild areas and alter the existing natural balance of species. However, it seems crazy to attempt to 'freeze' the wild population at some arbitrary moment, especially as the flora has been already so depleted. Saving species in the garden and reintroducing or reinforcing natural wild populations is surely a sensible alternative, if done with proper care and forethought. It is important, for instance, to use only endemic kinds in the garden and in the wild, for original British species may differ in various features from Continental counterparts of the same plant.

Conserving our wild flora is a laudable objective. We can all help by trying to protect valuable sites and persuading local authorities and others to take an enlightened view when interests conflict. Churchyards and similar places are now being looked on as possible wild flower sanctuaries and this too can be encouraged. Even schools can become centres for saving wild flowers – something that can be done along with the educational message.

Most plants included in this book are not in immediate danger of extinction, but many are still becoming scarcer. There comes a point when plants struggle to maintain populations, as a lively genetic pool is essential for a species to remain healthily active. Gardeners can help here, even by growing plants that appear quite plentiful in the wild. There are, in addition, huge numbers of interesting British flowers which have not been mentioned. Reading a good modern flora and joining a local society will reveal species that may be in need of protection and encouragement, both nationally and locally.

After decades of major losses, there is now a chance – maybe a last chance – to halt the decline and possibly even improve the

Early purple orchid, *Orchis mascula*, is still quite common

situation. Even those plants not at risk of extinction may well be in this category at a local or county level. It is a reproach to us all that so many plants known as 'common x or y' are no longer common.

The Wildlife and Countryside Act of 1981 gives legal protection to all wild plants. The list of totally protected plants is reviewed constantly by the Nature Conservancy Council and currently covers about one hundred species. It is an offence to pick, despoil or dig these up. A much longer list of threatened species is catalogued in the *British Red Data Book 1: Vascular Plants*, published by the Royal Society for Nature Conservation.

Further Information

SUPPLIERS OF PLANTS AND SEEDS

Many nurserymen, especially alpine and bulb specialists, list some native species and most of the large seedhouses now retail wild flower seed in shops. Seed of alpine plants is obtainable from the Alpine Garden Society. Some major suppliers of plants and sources of more unusual kinds of seed are given below.

Invaluable for all gardeners is *The Plant Finder*, published by the RHS. It lists over 40,000 plants and the nurseries from which they may be purchased.

Ashton Wold Wild Flowers Ashton Wold, Nr Oundle, Peterborough PE8 5LZ – plants and seeds.

John Chambers 15 Westleigh Rd, Barton Seagrave, Kettering, Northants NN15 5AJ – plants in collections and seeds.

Chiltern Seeds Bortree Stile, Ulverston, Cumbria LA12 7PB – seeds of native and exotic species.

Emorsgate Seeds Donald MacIntyre, Terrington Court, Terrington St Clement, Kings Lynn, Norfolk PE34 4NT – plants and seeds.

Kingsfield Tree Nursery G & J E Peacock, Broadenham Lane, Winsham, Chard, Somerset TA20 4JF – plants including trees.

NPK Landlife Ltd 542 Parrs Wood Rd, East Didsbury, Manchester M20 0QA – plants.

Oak Cottage Herb Farm, Ruth Thompson, Nesscliffe, Salop DY4 1DB – plants, mainly herbs.

Suffolk Herbs Ltd Sawyers Farm, Little Cornard, Sudbury, Suffolk CO10 0NY – seeds including herbs.

W. W. Johnson & Son Ltd London Rd, Boston, Lincs PE21 8AD – seeds including grasses.

A path through corn cockles and poppies

SOCIETIES

Local libraries have addresses of natural history societies in the area and of county naturalist trusts. If you have difficulty, write to:
Council for Nature, c/o Zoological Gardens, Regent's Park, London NW1 4RY.

Botanical Society of the British Isles, c/o British Museum (Natural History), Cromwell Rd, London SW7 5BD. (the most heavyweight society)

Botanical Society of Edinburgh, Botany Dept, University of Edinburgh, Mayfield Rd, Edinburgh EH9 3JH (Scottish wild plants)

British Butterfly Conservation Society, Tudor House, Quorn, Loughborough, Leics LE12 8AD

British Pteridological Society, 42 Lewisham Rd, Smethwick, Warley, W Midlands B66 2BS (ferns)

Council for the Protection of Rural England, 4 Hobart Place, London SW1W 0HY

Council for the Protection of Rural Wales, 14 Broad St, Welshpool, Powys SY21 7SD

Farming and Wildlife Group, The Lodge, Sandy, Beds SG19 2DL

Fauna and Flora Preservation Society, 8–12 Camden High St, London NW1 0JN

Field Studies Council, 9 Devereux Court, Strand, London WC2R 3JR

Hardy Plant Society, 10 St Barnabas Rd, Emner Green, Reading, Berks

Herb Society, 77 Great Peter St, London SW1P 2EZ

National Council for the Conservation of Plants and Gardens, The Pines, RHS Garden, Wisley, Woking, Surrey GU23 6QB

Nature Conservancy Council, Northminster House, Northminster Rd, Peterborough PE1 1AV

Royal Horticultural Society, PO Box 313, Vincent Square, London SW1P 2PE

Royal Society for Nature Conservation, 22 The Green, Nettleham, Lincoln LN2 2NR

Royal Society for the Protection of Birds, The Lodge, Sandy, Beds SG19 2DL

Scottish Field Studies Association, 158 Craigcrook Rd, Edinburgh EH4 3PP

Wild Flower Society, 68 Outwoods Rd, Loughborough, Leics LE11 3LY (amateur; useful for those new to wild flower study)

Woodland Trust, Autumn Park, Dysart Rd, Grantham, Lincs NG31 6LL

Index

Page numbers in **bold** refer to illustrations

I Recommended Plants

N.B. 1. Propagation methods are indicated as follows: S = seed/spore;
D = Division; C = Cuttings; R = Root cuttings; B = Buy, initially.
2. (P) after the name of a plant indicates that it is on the protected list
(see p. 57)

II Other Plants Mentioned